by
Robin Emmerson

CHURCH HOUSE PUBLISHING
Great Smith Street, London SW1P 3NZ

ISBN 0 7151 7550 5

First published 1991

The publication of this book has been aided by the Worshipful Company of Goldsmiths of London.
The author wishes to thank the following for making this little book possible and improving it in so many ways:
David Beasley
Claude Blair
Donald Findlay
the late Revd Canon James Gilchrist
Philippa Glanville
Jonathan Goodchild
Susan Hare
the Revd Canon Peter Hawker
Ronald Homer
the Revd Canon David Sharpe
the Very Revd Henry Stapleton
David Williams
Nigel Yates

For permission to reproduce photographs gratitude is expressed to the Worshipful Company of Goldsmiths of London (nos 2, 3, 6, 12, 13, 15, 17-19, 21, 22), the Dean and Chapter of Durham Cathedral (colour plate C), the Dean and Chapter of Westminster Abbey (no. 18), the Sainsbury Centre at the University of East Anglia (colour plate B), the Victoria and Albert Museum (cover and nos 1, 4, 5, 7-9, 11, 14), and the Pierpont Morgan Library, New York (colour plate A).
The drawings are by June Emmerson.

Designed and Produced by:
The Creative House, Saffron Walden, Essex.

Cover: Silver of the mid-seventeenth century from Staunton Harold, Leicestershire, in the Victoria and Albert Museum. The church is in the care of the National Trust.

Preface

Worshippers of every religion, every culture, every country and every age have felt that they must offer to their creator only what is best. Christianity is no exception and with the service of Holy Communion as its centrepiece, its vessels, such as the chalice, are to be of the best design, material and workmanship. Christianity is, however, a living religion. The way people worship is continually evolving, and over the centuries the design of church plate has changed accordingly. Just as at table we no longer customarily drink from silver or pewter tankards, so some old church plate has gone out of use. Such objects cannot be discarded. They have been used in worship, they are old, they are beautiful, so they are put away in a safe. When discovered later their material value excites a temptation to convert them into cash. But it is not this generation's right so to dispose of historical and traditional objects of previous generations' generosity.

It was in order to display the many articles of plate which would otherwise be hidden in a safe or bank vault that the Goldsmiths' Company has set up treasuries where such plate can be displayed. The purpose of Robin Emmerson's book is to provide a guide to church plate, both in the treasuries and the parish churches, and to explain the various articles to be found there. I hope that this will encourage a greater appreciation of our inheritance and inspire more people to present to their churches examples of modern workmanship of similar quality and beauty.

Dr. C. E. Gordon Smith
Prime Warden of the Goldsmiths' Company

CHURCH PLATE

In your town or village, is there anywhere that still has silver which was made for that place three or four hundred years ago? Probably not in any of the grand houses, but very likely in the church. Household silver was always liable to be melted down and remade according to the changing fashion in dining and other domestic habits. In a crisis like the Civil War or an accumulation of gambling debts it was sold for the value of the metal. Church plate has, at least since Elizabethan times, been exposed to fewer risks. It therefore has great value as a living witness to the past of local communities. It may also shed unexpected light on life beyond the church door, when we find some obsolete household object like a posset-pot or a porringer preserved because it was given for a different use in church. Most of all, one is impressed by the continuity of worship in the Church of England, the fact that so many parishes have been using the same silver cup for communion ever since it was made in the sixteenth century. These are precious vessels indeed.

The most important use for silver in church was and is the service in which Christians commemorate the Last Supper that Jesus had with his disciples before he was crucified. They eat bread and drink wine over which these words have been spoken: 'This is my body' and 'This is my blood – do this in remembrance of me'. The service has been known by many names including Holy Communion, the Mass, the Lord's Supper and the Eucharist. Ever since the Middle Ages the Church has insisted that the vessels for the bread and wine should be of worthy material such as silver. The origin of this should be seen in the normal mediaeval tendency to rate the arts in importance according to the cost of their ingredients. Since God must have the best vessels, they should be made of the best materials, that is, the most precious.

Cup from the Water Newton hoard, fourth century, in the British Museum

Chalice from Trewhiddle, Cornwall, ninth century, in the British Museum

*Head of crozier,
thirteenth century*

Of course at no time has church plate all been of silver or gold even for the communion vessels. Other materials including pewter, brass, wood and glass have been used, although the term 'plate' really suggests metalwares. It ought to be pointed out that 'plate' and 'plate*d*' have quite different meanings: 'silver-plated' means made of base metal and coated with a thin layer of silver. Some silver-plated things are church plate, but not all church plate is silver-plated!

The makers of silver have generally called themselves goldsmiths because they work in both metals, and since the Middle Ages the Goldsmiths' Company of London has exercised a general control over the trade in England. At a time when the nation's coinage was supposed to be specific weights of silver and gold, objects made of these metals were a form of currency in themselves, and it was vital to ensure the standard of purity. This was done by *assaying*[1] or testing each piece, and those passed as of sterling standard were struck with a *hallmark*. It is worth emphasising that this was and is a guarantee of the purity of the metal, not of the quality of workmanship.

1 Words in italics are explained in the Glossary

The Middle Ages

Before 1200 many churches did not possess even a *chalice* of silver, but by 1500 most had not only that but a good deal more besides. Almost all church silver was melted down during the upheavals of the *Reformation* in the sixteenth century. Pre-Reformation chalices and *patens* are therefore very rare. Chalices in 1500 had a tall stem with a swelling half way down it called a knop or knot. The bowl was relatively small, and there was a spreading foot to make the tall vessel stable. This shape was prescribed by the Church. The knop was for the priest to grasp when he lifted the chalice high up at the point in the service where he consecrated the wine. The bowl did not need to be large because only the priest was allowed to drink the consecrated wine. The foot of the chalice at this period was angular rather than round, because it was the custom at the end of the service to drain the chalice on its side. With a round foot there was a risk that it might roll off on to the floor. The bread used at Mass was in the form of small wafers, and the special plate for them known as a paten was therefore quite small. A paten was usually made with a chalice and was designed to sit on the chalice, so that when a mediaeval inventory lists a chalice one should assume a paten as well.

A priest in the Middle Ages was generally buried with a real or imitation chalice and paten. Bishops might be buried with silver ones. This is how most of the earliest chalices, like the twelfth-century one from Archbishop Walter's tomb in Canterbury Cathedral, have been preserved. For most priests a pewter one or even a wax model had to suffice. By the fourteenth century pewter chalices were regarded as unworthy for Mass, but they continued to be made for burial purposes.

Archbishop Walter's chalice, late twelfth century, in Canterbury Cathedral

Incense boat from Ramsey Abbey, fourteenth century, in the Victoria and Albert Museum

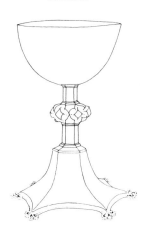

Chalice, about 1500

1.
Chalice and paten, 1479 from Nettlecombe, Somerset in the Victoria and Albert Museum

From the Reformation to the Civil War

Mediaeval churches were prepared in a real emergency to consign their treasures to the melting-pot for capital. Unfortunately for them the King in the eleventh and twelfth centuries often shared this attitude to their property. After 1200 there were no more royal confiscations, and this probably explains why the bishops at last succeeded in persuading most parishes to acquire a silver chalice. Parliaments in the late Middle Ages regularly suggested, when the King asked them for money, that he plunder the wealth of the churches, but it was not until the 1530s that this became a reality.

In 1517 Martin Luther in Germany declared a clean break from the mediaeval church, with its services in Latin and its cult of saints and relics. His followers became known as Protestants, and by 1530 they included a number of Englishmen. When Henry VIII broke with Rome in 1534 however, the immediate cause was not a matter of faith. It was simply that the Pope would not let him divorce Catherine of Aragon and marry Anne Boleyn. Once free of papal authority and himself established as 'Supreme Head in earth of the Church of England' Henry could do as he pleased. His minister Thomas Cromwell saw that the rising tide of Protestant opposition to monks and the cult of relics could be used to the advantage of the Treasury. The monasteries were dissolved and their goods confiscated by the Crown. Many cathedrals were monasteries, but even those which were not lost their shrines and much plate. In the 1540s it was the turn of collegiate churches and chantry chapels, many of which were in parish churches. At this point many parishes realised that their own plate was threatened, and there began a quiet scramble to liquidate these assets before the King could get at them.

*Edward VI
communion cup*

The death of Henry in 1547 and the ascendancy of the Protestants under Edward VI left no doubt about it. The most ominous sign was the appointment in 1549 of commissions to make an inventory of church goods in each county. In 1551 the Commissioners received orders to take from each parish everything but its least valuable chalice and paten.

Under the Protestant reformers all the old church vessels except chalices and patens were thus swept away, ostensibly as part of 'Popish superstition'. Services were now to be in English, and the service of the Lord's Supper became a feast which the congregation shared. They were allowed to drink the consecrated wine, and the 1552 Prayer Book recommended the use of ordinary bread instead of wafers.

There are 18 cups surviving which were made for the new communion service in the reign of Edward VI (1547-53). They are the first English church plate of distinctively Protestant form. In shape the new *communion cups* are like household wine-cups and quite different from chalices. Gone are the large knop on the stem and the small bowl. The new cups have deep and capacious bowls. Some have a paten which when turned upside down fits the cup as a cover, its foot doing double duty as a handle. The obvious purpose of these large and heavy cups was to hold enough wine for the congregation but in some cases there may have been also a financial motive. Parishes knew that the King would leave them only one drinking vessel. If they melted down two chalices to make one large cup, they could save the silver of one chalice from the royal clutches.

Under Queen Mary (1553-58) there was a brief return to Roman Catholicism, but with the accession of Elizabeth the process of Protestant reform continued. Every parish was now ordered to change its remaining chalice for one of the new-style communion cups. The motive was not quite as obvious as it appears. The Elizabethan Church followed a moderate brand of Protestantism, and many similar churches on the Continent were happy to use their old chalices for the new service. But the Roman Catholic William Alleyn noted that in England in the 1560s 'Many priests said mass secretly and celebrated the heretical (i.e. Protestant) offices and supper in public'. For the Roman Catholic mass they needed a chalice; one of the new communion cups would not do. Taking their chalices away was therefore an effective way of stopping the old service.

London communion cup, 1560s

Communion cup and cover, made in Norwich about 1568

2.
(Far left) Communion cup and cover, 1549 from St Mary Aldermary, London in the Victoria and Albert Museum

3.
(Left) Pair of flagons from Rendcombe, Gloucestershire, 1592

Flagon, made in London,
1572-3, Wells Cathedral

Communion cup
and cover, made in
Exeter about 1574

4.
(Right) Steeple cup,
1599 from Charing, Kent

5.
(Far right) Flagon, 1646
from Thirtleby, Yorkshire
in the Victoria and Albert
Museum

The order to change the chalices was given with careful timing to the dioceses in turn, presumably to prevent the goldsmiths from being overwhelmed by the amount of work. For the trade it was a godsend. Norwich foresaw the rush of orders and even set up its own hallmarking system to maintain standards and prevent unscrupulous undercutting. Between 1562 and 1576, and starting in the south-east, every diocese in England and Wales received its instructions. Surviving cups show that in most places the work was done within two or three years of the bishop's order. One reason for the efficiency was that poverty gave a parish no excuse: a small amount of the silver in a chalice would pay for making a communion cup out of the rest. For a poor parish with a small chalice, this could result in a cup too small for the congregation, with a bowl beaten out thin to make the silver go further. Elsewhere the parishioners often dug into their pockets to make sure that the cup would be sufficiently large and sturdy. Each cup was of course supposed to have its own combined paten and cover, replacing the mediaeval paten, but it seems to have taken a couple of years for this to be generally understood, so that most of the cups made between 1562 and 1564 were supplied without a paten-cover and were only equipped with one a few years later. [1]

Sacred imagery was now regarded as 'superstitious' so the engraved decoration on cups and covers usually takes the form of arabesque scrolls within strapwork, both novel forms of Renaissance ornament only recently brought to England. Norwich and Exeter, with their own prolific goldsmiths, produced excellent cups with distinctive local features: Norwich bowls tend to be broad and bell-shaped, sometimes

1 Charles Oman, *English Church Plate, 597-1830*, p161

with a pair of raised ribs running round the middle, while Exeter bowls generally possess a vertical lip set at an angle to the bowl. Everywhere from Chester to Cornwall the great conversion gave opportunities to local goldsmiths as well as to their London colleagues.

As it became common to use ordinary bread rather than wafers, a larger paten became desirable. Big patens which did not do duty as covers were known in London in Elizabeth's reign, and after 1600 their use spread. Most of them were dishes with a rim or sides, standing on a foot. In the 1630s a rare variety with its own domed cover appears, and these were still being made in the eighteenth century. Patens of all kinds, including the small pre-Reformation ones designed for wafer bread, frequently show surfaces scored with knife-marks, evidence that ordinary bread has been cut up on them. Everyone was supposed by law to take communion regularly in their parish church. Because of the large numbers, it became necessary to provide large jugs, known as *flagons* or more often just 'pots', to hold enough for the service. Often they were made and used in pairs. The oldest surviving one is at Wells Cathedral and dates from 1572. It has a pear-shaped body with a hinged cover, and stands on a stem and foot. The most usual sort is the cylindrical flagon, also with a hinged cover. Almost all those surviving were made after about 1600. Most examples of both kinds do not have a lip projecting at the front for pouring, but pour quite well without one. They follow the shapes of the household wine-jugs of the period. Because the wine was actually consecrated in the flagons, it was thought that they should be silver, but the amount of silver in a flagon made it too expensive for many parishes, who therefore used a pewter one. The Canons of 1604 directed that the wine 'be brought to the table in a sweet standing pot or stoup of pewter, if not of purer metal'.

Queen Elizabeth carefully steered a middle course between the old Catholic religion and the extreme Protestants known as Puritans, but after her death in 1603 the Church of England became increasingly divided into two hostile camps. Some wished to stress the continuity of the Church of England with the Church of earlier centuries. The most important figure amongst these was Lancelot Andrewes, Dean of Westminster at the time of Elizabeth's death in 1603, and subsequently Bishop in turn of Chichester, Ely and Winchester until his death in 1626. On the altar in his chapel he placed an *alms dish* flanked by a pair of candlesticks. Instead of communion cups, he favoured chalices of late mediaeval form. These innovations may not seem very startling nowadays, but to contemporaries used to an almost bare communion table they

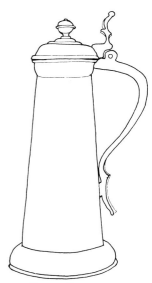

Pewter flagon, about 1610

Chalice and cover, about 1615

Flagon, about 1630

appeared either splendidly dignified or shockingly 'Popish'.

William Laud shared these ideas with Andrewes, and while he was Archbishop of Canterbury in the years leading up to the Civil War, they had considerable influence both upon cathedrals and upon many aristocratic supporters of Charles I. Andrewes's most important legacy, however, was the idea of the set of plate made to match, which was quickly taken up even by those who preferred less elaborate ritual.

Paten, about 1630

The Civil War saw very little looting of plate from parish churches, although some cathedrals suffered badly. During the Commonwealth a few owners of private chapels even commissioned plate of mediaeval inspiration as promoted by Andrewes, inspired by late mediaeval forms and decoration.

Pewter flagon,
about 1660

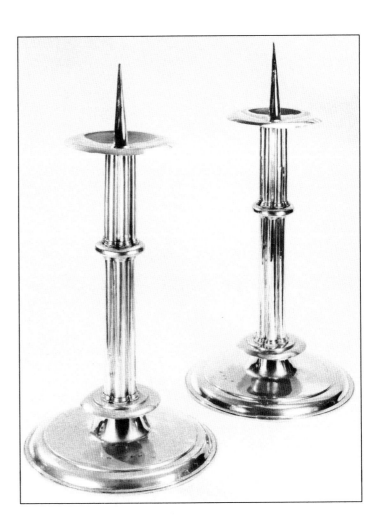

6.
Pair of pricket
candlesticks, 1661
in Gloucester Cathedral

From the Restoration to the Regency

At the Restoration of Charles II in 1660 candlesticks and alms-basins returned to the High Altar in cathedrals. Chalices of mediaeval inspiration were chosen for equipping the Chapel Royal. Such silver, sometimes inventive in form and richly decorated, was in contrast to the undecorated plate of basically Elizabethan type which was still being made for most churches. By 1700, however, we find the designs of chalices and communion cups coming closer together in deep rounded bowls and the baluster stems of the so-called 'Queen Anne' style.

It may seem puzzling that so many pieces of late seventeenth- and eighteenth-century communion plate, especially flagons, are so very large and heavy. In many parishes Holy Communion was held only twice a year, and such a special event guaranteed a large congregation, expecting to take a mouthful rather than a sip of wine.

The nature of church plate was subtly changing. During the previous century the cups and flagons used in church had been much the same as those used in well-to-do households. In Charles II's reign, however, domestic fashions changed. Drinking-glasses took the place of silver wine-cups, and it was no longer considered smart to display rows of gleaming flagons, now that meals were taken in more private rooms. The result was that church cups and flagons became, through no fault of their own, quite different from what anybody used at home. That the Church had no particular desire for this

Communion cup and cover, about 1670

Strainer spoon, about 1685

7.
(Far left) Communion cup and cover, 1663 from Pattishall, Northamptonshire

8.
(Left) Flagon, 1672 from Easton Maudit, Northamptonshire

Candlestick,
about 1690

Chalice,
about 1720

9.
Communion cup,
1707 from Deptford
Congregational Church,
in the Victoria and Albert
Museum

difference is shown by the changing shape of patens. The standard seventeenth-century form, a dish standing on a tall foot, was just like the domestic *salver* of the period. The domestic version had a rather different use: Thomas Blount in 1661 describes it thus: 'Salver . . . is a new fashioned piece of wrought plate, broad and flat, with a foot underneath, and is used in giving Beer, or other liquid thing to save the Carpit or Cloathes from drops'.[1] Some church plates and salvers were made to fit a matching flagon, and must therefore have been intended not as patens but as stands of this kind. Some eighteenth-century patens followed the form of dinner-plates or of the household trays on several small feet known as *waiters*. It is often difficult to know whether a particular silver or pewter dish was used as a paten or an almsdish. A clue may be provided by an inscription, or by knife marks showing that bread has been cut up on it. While cylindrical flagons remained the commonest type, those with pear-shaped bodies tended to be particularly well-made and to owe something to the fashionable design of items like coffee pots. Some churches had a huge pewter flagon, not for the altar, but especially for the bellringers to slake their thirst.

It is therefore often difficult to distinguish between pieces made for a church and household objects which were given to a church at some later date. Other gifts are of obvious domestic origin. Some very grand cups and flagons were given to churches after they had become too unfashionable for the dining table. This is fortunate for posterity, because otherwise their owners would certainly have consigned them to the melting-pot to pay for some more fashionable silver like a set of sauceboats. Sometimes rather surprising things were given. What would a church do with a two-handled covered bowl or a cup with a long snakelike spout? It is difficult

1 Quoted in Charles Oman, *English Domestic Silver* (1968 ed.), p132

enough to be sure of their original domestic function. The former may be what is described in old inventories as a cup for caudle or posset, richly spiced combinations of ale with milk or egg-yolks. The latter was probably made for syllabub. At Parham, Suffolk, the church plate included a squeezer of the sort normally used for oranges or lemons in making punch. There was always a risk that the churchwardens might use the sacred vessels for refreshments at their vestry meetings – hence the occasional inscription like that engraved on a flagon from Okeford Fitzpaine in Dorset: 'To be by them us'd onely in the sacrament of the Lord's Supper'. The communion wine, however, often needed straining to remove impurities, for bottling was a new and uncertain science, and much wine was still bought in cask. The straining could be done by means of a spoon, often with perforations in the bowl. Some parishes also possess an eighteenth-century knife which was used for cutting ordinary bread on the paten. These are just like the knives one would have found on a Georgian dining-table. One eighteenth-century innovation was the silver 'collecting shoe', a container which was partly

Flagon,
about 1740

10.
Holy Communion,
from Introduction to
the Sacrament
by L. Addison, 1693.

*Recusant pyx,
about 1610*

*Recusant chalice,
about 1640*

*Recusant monstrance,
about 1750*

11.
*Sick communion set
by Robert Hennell, 1823,
Victoria and Albert
Museum*

covered so that the amount of money people gave was discreetly concealed. Large or wealthy parishes sometimes had staves with silver emblems on top for the verger or churchwardens to carry in processions.

When one compares it with the marvellous domestic silver of the time, most eighteenth-century church plate looks rather unoriginal in design. There are sadly few pieces which are beautifully decorated in the style of the period like the exquisite Rococo set made for Durham cathedral in 1767 by Francis Butty and Nicholas Dumée. One underlying reason must be the infrequency with which the service of Holy Communion was held in many parishes. Religious enthusiasms were directed elsewhere, and it was not likely that the sermons of John Wesley would have a great effect on church plate. The eighteenth-century revival of personal faith did, however, affect the provision of Holy Communion for the sick. Miniature communion cups and patens for ministering to the sick in their own homes were already in use in London's newly fashionable West End in the late seventeenth century: the earliest surviving was made for St James Piccadilly in 1683. Because a clergyman could perform the service in any private house without having to ask permission from the parish priest, we find Charles Wesley in the 1740s making considerable use of it as part of his ministry. The practice was widely adopted, and by 1800 we find miniature sets being made comprising cup, paten and flagon or silver-topped glass bottle. They remained popular in Victorian times.

Anglicans were not the only Christians for whom church plate was made in the seventeenth and eighteenth centuries. Roman Catholics, known as *Recusants* from their refusal to

A. *Fifteenth-century Mass from the Hours of Catherine of Cleves.*
The Pierpont Morgan Library, New York. M.945, f143

B. *Silver-gilt flagon engraved in the style of Nicaise Roussel, 1607
Norwich Cathedral Treasury (from Westacre).*

C. Silver-gilt flagon by Butty & Dumée, 1767
from Durham Cathedral

D. Chalice, designed by Butterfield and made by J. Keith, 1854

take the Protestant communion in their parish churches, heard the Roman mass in private, at first in conditions of the greatest secrecy, for discovery could mean death. Seventeenth-century Recusant chalices were therefore often made to come to pieces so that they could be more easily concealed. The goldsmith dare not put his mark on them, let alone take them to be assayed, so they are difficult to date. From the seventeenth century only chalices, patens, *pyxes* and *cruets* survive, but after 1700 life was less hazardous for Catholics, and a full range of eighteenth-century plate for the Roman mass survives, most of it hallmarked.

The more extreme Protestant churches on the Continent which followed Calvin used sets of beakers for communion. A set of four survives which was made for the church of the Dutch immigrants in Norwich in the 1570s. Nonconformist Protestants regarded the Lord's Supper very much as a shared feast, and their seventeenth-century plate is often actual domestic tableware, with pewter plates and large sets of silver cups.

Recusant sanctuary lamp, about 1720

Recusant ciborium, about 1710.

12.
Oval almsdish in silver-gilt by Edward Yorke, 1710

Victorian and Twentieth Century

Chalice,
about 1870

Victorian England experienced a religious revolution which, so far as church plate and ritual are concerned, went in the opposite direction from its sixteenth-century predecessor. The Oxford Movement was a phenomenon of the 1830s, but left a lasting influence. It was sparked off by Government attempts to reform the Anglican Church in Ireland. Reform was in fact long overdue, but to some English churchmen this brought to a head the need for greater reverence for the Church of England and its institutions. Men like Keble, Newman and Pusey saw that in many ways the Church had become lax, and were passionately opposed to mere 'paper religion'. They invoked the values of the past in the same romantic spirit as the revivers of chivalric ideals and of Gothic architecture in the same decade. Their ideas were taken up and applied to the physical trappings of worship in 1839 by the Cambridge Camden (later Ecclesiological) Society. It was little wonder therefore that the Society saw a return to the Middle Ages as the way to restore dignity to worship. The architect-designer A.W.N. Pugin was already having Gothic church plate made to his design by Hardman's of Birmingham. He believed Gothic to be the only style appropriate for a Christian country, and he joined the Roman Catholic Church. His publications, from *Contrasts* (1836) onwards, were polemical and influential. The Ecclesiological Society saw themselves to some extent as his competitors. It was an article in their journal *The Ecclesiologist* in 1842 by the architect William Butterfield which really began the revival of mediaeval plate in the Church of England. They were particularly concerned to avoid those designs of Pugin which were derived from Continental rather than English Gothic. It was most important to be able to show an English precedent in order to avoid the charge of imitating Continental Roman Catholicism, for anything 'Romish' would meet with popular disapproval. The English Protestant fear of Rome was still strong. Those who favoured the new, more elaborate kind of service became known as Ritualists as opposed to those who kept to the eighteenth-century way of worship.

The Ritualists preferred chalices to communion cups, and less wine was drunk because people were given only a sip in order to make them realise that the Sacrament was precious. With the chalice the small paten was reintroduced, although wafer bread was rather slower to follow. The massive flagons of the past were frowned upon. Since a flagon of smaller capacity was still needed, and flagons had not been used in the mediaeval Church, one of the only two surviving mediaeval English silver *cruets* was recommended as a model. It is preserved at St Peter Port, Guernsey, and dates from about 1525. Unfortunately it has a long snake-like spout which makes it difficult to wash clean after use. The design was therefore generally adapted by replacing the spout with a simple pouring lip projecting in front, and in this form it became the standard Victorian Gothic flagon.

One problem with the new chalices was that many were unstable because there was not enough weight of silver in them. Thanks to the Industrial Revolution, silver could now be made in thin, even sheets which were then formed into vessels by 'spinning' on a lathe. Using less silver kept prices down, and there was therefore a general tendency to make things too lightweight. The Ecclesiological Society did not help matters because, instead of looking at machine production in Birmingham, they were entranced by visions of the Holy Grail studded with jewels: 'If indeed we were able to have a perfectly plain chalice and might lay out an unlimited sum on it, we should, perhaps, prefer greater weight of metal as the more valuable; but the money laid out on this is preferably spent on enrichments – or on jewelry – and the like'.[1] Solid Elizabethan communion cups were sometimes melted down to create these insubstantial visions of the Middle Ages. The best architect-designers like Pugin, Butterfield, Burges and Street were careful to avoid such faults and produced superb pieces with their own original character. Enamelling techniques which had not been seen

Flagon,
about 1860

Cruet, about 1525,
St. Peter Port, Guernsey

13.
Flagon, chalice and paten
by Edward Barnard
& Sons, 1831

1 Quoted in James Gilchrist, *Anglican Church Plate*, pp83-4

19

since the Middle Ages enjoyed a colourful revival. Unfortunately imaginative work of this kind is very much in the minority, and big firms of ecclesiastical furnishers were soon beginning to dictate taste by the standard nature of their goods.

It is difficult now to imagine the furore that could be created a hundred years ago by a cross and a pair of candlesticks on an altar, but many English parishes had not seen this sight since the sixteenth century, and it was associated with the 'foreign superstition' of Rome. In this context practices like the burning of incense were also seen as a return to Catholicism: 'Mr Punch's ABC for Youthful Anglicans' in 1871, calling a *censer* by its grander name of thurible, says:

'T is the Thurible, whose very smell
incenses the people, and makes them rebel'.[1]

By the 1880s, however, the Ritualists were becoming bolder. They even began to reserve consecrated wafer bread in a *pyx*. The pressure of opposition made them continue to seek the authority of precedent for everything they did, and as a result they became rigidly doctrinaire. They diverged into two camps, one copying English churches before the Reformation, and the other following recent Roman Catholic practice on the Continent. The mediaevalists now based their ideas strictly on the instruction in the Prayer Book that the ornaments in church should remain as they were in the second year of Edward VI's reign. It took a lot of scholarly work to discover what these had been! Their textbook was J.T. Micklethwaite's *The Ornaments of the Rubric* (1901) but his

14.
(Right) Chalice designed by A. W. N. Pugin, made by Hardman & Co, 1849, Victoria and Albert Museum

15.
(Far right) Chalice designed by Willam Burges, made by Hardman & Co, 1862

1 Punch, 8th April 1871, quoted in Anson *Fashions in Church Furnishings 1840-1940*, p215

ideas were already being popularized by Percy Dearmer in *The Parson's Handbook* (1899). Their rivals accused them of 'British Museum Religion', appealing instead to the living traditions of ritual as it had survived on the Continent. Churches of this persuasion were likely to have as many as six candlesticks on the altar. Their pressure group was the Society of St Peter and St Paul, founded in 1911. They had the advantage of being able to import from abroad the Roman Catholic vessels they favoured, whereas the mediaevalists had to make do with modern copies of what they admired.

This doctrinaire approach clearly did not leave much room for original ideas in the design of church plate. The root of the problem was that the nineteenth century was reeling under the impact of the changes brought about by industrialization. The ritualists were seeking the authority of a tradition of worship for the same reason that the architects were copying past styles – in order to create a comforting illusion of security in a world that was changing very fast.

16.
Nineteenth-century Ritualistic Eucharist, illustrated in The Directorium Anglicanum, *1865*

Plate itself reflected these changes. In the mid-eighteenth century it was discovered how to produce a composite metal – 'Sheffield Plate' – by rolling out, under heat, a sheet of copper sandwiched between two thin sheets of silver, and this was sometimes used for church plate. In the 1840s Elkingtons developed the alternative technique of *electroplating*, which enabled finished metal objects of any shape to be plated with other metals, especially silver. The increasing ability of industry to make its products look like something else brought an artistic reaction in favour of 'truth to materials' and 'honesty'. These ideals were embodied in the work of the Arts and Crafts Movement, begun by William Morris. Percy Dearmer stated that church vessels should show evidence of Christian values. He was thinking especially of the 'sweatshop' working conditions in many Victorian factories. Eric Gill stated bluntly: 'The products of industrialism are unsuitable for the furnishing of churches'. [1]

Morris and his followers wanted a world where every worker could take pleasure in his work and become, in effect, a craftsman. The result towards the end of the century was not the end of drudgery on the production line but the emergence of artist-craftsmen like Henry Wilson or John Paul Cooper, men

17.
Chalice by
Henry Wilson,
1900 in Gloucester
Cathedral

1 Architectural Review, July 1927, quoted in Anson, p 328

whose originality brought new life to the design of plate. Instead of polishing their work completely smooth, they would proudly leave the hammer-marks showing to prove that it was hand-made. Many of these people taught in art schools, and their influence in the long term was out of all proportion to the relatively small part they played in commercial terms.

In the years between the First and Second World Wars, new ideas from the Continent dealt the Arts and Crafts Movement a severe blow – first the jazzy style now called Art Deco, and then the 'functional design' of the modern architects. Neither had much impact on church plate at the time, but the functionalists had the effect of making people more receptive to new ideas when church plate began to be ordered again

18.
(Left) One of
four almsdishes by
Omar Ramsden for
Westminster Abbey,
1927

19.
(Below) Flagon by
R. E. Stone, 1954

after 1945. Their ideas were well suited to the new movement in the Church towards simplicity in worship. Arts and Crafts ideals survived between the wars in the work of influential silversmiths and teachers like Harold Stabler and Bernard Cuzner. In Scandinavia, which was late in industrializing and had no history of opposition between art and industry, these ideas were adapted to factory production by George Jensen and his pupils. This continuity enabled what one critic has called 'the precious vessel of handicraft aesthetics' to be handed on to a new generation of craftsmen after 1945.

Silver has therefore been able to share in that rebirth of the crafts which is the most important fact in the history of British decorative art since the Second World War. The roots of this lie in a reaction against modern mechanized living: we need to feel the marks of human workmanship, just as we need to maintain contact with nature. It is because good craftsmanship reminds us of human capacities and limitations that it is so suitable for use in worship. The bulk of church plate, however, continues to be mass-produced work sold by the big firms of ecclesiastical furnishers. This monotony is mostly the fault of timid customers. Silver by leading craftsmen like Leslie Durbin and Gerald Benney shows that postwar silver can be as inspiring as that of earlier centuries.

20.
Modern Eucharist at
St Peter Mancroft Church,
Norwich

Some art schools like Medway and the Sir John Cass are currently producing excellent and inventive young silversmiths who would love the chance to work for the Church. The Goldsmiths' Company does much to foster and promote the work of contemporary silversmiths, and runs a special commissioning service to help customers find the right craftsman and obtain good quality vessels to suit their needs.

In keeping with the movement towards simplicity in worship is the idea that good craftsmanship matters more than precious materials. This has resulted in some good work, such as altar sets of cross and candlesticks in mild steel, and communion vessels of pottery. Unfortunately the nature of these materials is such that they are less likely than silver to survive in good condition for future generations to use and enjoy.

21.
*Head of
St Michael's staff
by Leslie Durbin, 1960
in Gloucester Cathedral*

22.
Chalice and flagon
by Simon Beer,
1980 in
Southwark Cathedral

23.
Two chalices and patens
by Melanie Sproat, 1985
in Durham Cathedral

Where to See Church Plate

The Goldsmiths' Company has funded the creation of treasuries in a number of dioceses, mostly in cathedrals. These are permanent displays of plate on loan from churches in the diocese. The display in the Victoria and Albert Museum gives the best general coverage of church plate, but many regional museums have notable examples from their area. The Librarian at Goldsmiths' Hall would be grateful to hear of smaller museums which hold interesting church plate.

Diocesan Treasuries mainly funded by the Goldsmiths' Company

Lincoln	Oxford
Winchester	Gloucester
Norwich	Canterbury
York	Peterborough
Chichester	London, St Paul's

Independent Treasuries to which the Goldsmiths' Company has made financial grants

Ripon	St Albans
Durham	Carlisle
Hereford	Salisbury
Newark, parish church	London, Westminster Abbey
Lichfield, St Mary (redundant church)	

Independent Treasuries which received no grant from the Goldsmiths

Bristol, St Nicholas (redundant church)
Norwich, St Peter Mancroft

Some treasuries display vestments as well as plate. Vestments originated in the late Roman period as simply a smart version of ordinary masculine dress, the equivalent of a 'Sunday best' suit. Gradually this outfit became standardized into a uniform, while fashions in ordinary dress became completely different. The process is familiar to us from the survival of the eighteenth-century wig in the courtroom, or the Victorian bonnet worn by Salvation Army ladies.

At the Reformation in the sixteenth century, rich vestments were abolished in the Church of England, but they made a controversial return in Victorian times. The various garments worn as vestments by modern priests are therefore basically the same as those worn by mediaeval priests. The most important, worn when celebrating the *Eucharist*, is the *chasuble*, a cloak with a hole to go over the head. Other vestments are explained under the names in the glossary.

Glossary

Words in *italics* are included in the list

Agnus Dei	'Lamb of God' in Latin. The lamb stands for Christ as the victim sacrificed for mankind.
Alb	Long lightweight white robe with narrow sleeves worn under *chasuble*.
Almsdish	Dish for receiving the collection from the congregation.
Almuce	Fur cape worn under cope in the Middle Ages.
Alpha and Omega	First and last letters of the Greek alphabet, symbolizing God as the beginning and end of all things.
Amice	White neckcloth sometimes decorated with an *apparel*, part of the *Eucharistic vestments*.
Ampullae	Containers for the holy oils used at baptism, confirmation and in anointing the sick.
Apparels	Decorative rectangular panels of embroidery or brocade on an *alb* or *amice*.
Aspergillum	Sprinkler for holy water.
Assay	The testing of gold and silver articles for the purity of metal.
Aumbry	A lockable cupboard near the altar where the *Reserved Sacrament* may be kept.
Britannia Metal	Alloy of tin, antimony and copper used from about 1780 and designed to be rolled, pressed or spun rather than cast. Britannia ware is thus lighter and thinner than *pewter*.
	Electroplated Britannia Metal (EPBM) occurs from the 1840s onwards. Britannia Metal should not be confused with 'Britannia standard' silver.
Britannia standard	More correctly called the 'new sterling' standard, the required standard of purity for silver from 1697 to 1719, and available ever since as an alternative option to the *sterling standard*. The 'new sterling' standard is 95.84% fine silver.
Burse	Stiffened brocade case for a *corporal*.

Censer	Incense burner, usually swung on chains held in the hand.
Chalice	Cup for wine at the *Eucharist*. Chalices have been of many shapes over the centuries, and the term really indicates that the cup is special rather than that it is of a particular shape.
Chalice spoon	Used in the Middle Ages for adding a drop of water to the wine in the *chalice*.
Chalice veil	Cover for *chalice* when sitting on the altar but not actually in use.
Chasuble	Cloak of circular or oval shape worn by the priest at the *Eucharist*.
Chi-Rho	The first two letters (XP) of 'Christ' in Greek.
Chrismatory	A box for *ampullae*.
Ciborium	Covered cup fitted with a lid, containing consecrated wafer bread.
Communion cup	Wine cup for the *Eucharist*, introduced by Protestants in the sixteenth century. It resembles a household cup to show that the wine is for the people as well as the priest.
Cope	Long cape opening at the front, worn especially for processions.
Corporal	Cloth placed on the altar for the sacred vessels to rest upon at the *Eucharist*.
Crozier	Staff in the form of a stylized shepherd's crook, carried by a bishop.
Cruets	Small jugs for wine and water, used in pairs at the *Eucharist*.
Electroplate	Plating base metals with silver by electrolysis, a technique developed by Elkingtons of Birmingham in the 1840s. The usual base metal was nickel silver, an alloy of copper, zinc and nickel. See also *Britannia Metal*.
Eucharist	The service which re-enacts the sharing of bread and wine at the Last Supper. Also known as the Mass, Holy Communion and the Lord's Supper.

Eucharistic vessels	Containers used at the *Eucharist*, principally *chalice* or *communion cup*, *paten* and *cruets* or *flagons*.
Eucharistic vestments	Special clothes worn by the priest at the *Eucharist*: *amice*, *alb*, *stole*, *maniple* and *chasuble*.
Ewer	Jug for water, used by the priest for washing at the *Eucharist*, or to hold water for baptisms.
Flagon	Jug for the wine for the *Eucharist*.
Funerary Chalice	*Chalice*, often of pewter, buried with a priest in the Middle Ages and often specially made for the purpose.
Gothic	The style of art in England between about 1200 and 1500. Most easily recognised by the use of pointed arches, it was revived in the nineteenth century.
Hallmarking	The official marking of silver and gold articles to show that their metal is sufficiently pure. The hall of the London Goldsmiths' Company was the first place where they were applied. Marks are struck with a metal punch, and the following may be found: the hallmark of the town of *assay*, *sterling* or *Britannia standard* marks, a date-letter showing the year of *assay*, and a maker's mark. There may also be the mark of the sovereign's head, used from 1784 to 1890 to indicate that duty on the article had been paid to the Government. It is not usually possible to identify the maker of a piece with a London hallmark before 1697.
Host	Wafer bread, consecrated at the *Eucharist*.
Huguenots	French Protestants. Those expelled from the French dominions in 1685 by the Revocation of the Edict of Nantes included craftsmen who then came to England and caused a revolution in the style of English silver.
Lamb of God	see *Agnus Dei*.
Maniple	Short scarf or napkin worn over the left wrist as part of the *Eucharistic vestments*.
Mitre	Special head-dress worn by bishops and archbishops (and some abbots in the Middle Ages).
Monstrance	Glass-fronted container for displaying the *Host*, set on a tall stem.

Ormolu	Gilt bronze, in its original form 'fire' or 'mercury' gilded, that is by coating it with an amalgam of gold and mercury under heat and evaporating the mercury.
Pall	(a) see *Pallium*. (b) a small linen towel folded in three for covering the *chalice*. (c) cloth covering a coffin, funeral bier or tomb.
Pallium	A strip of material worn around the neck with a strip hanging down from it before and behind. Worn by archbishops over the *chasuble*.
Parcel gilt	Partly gilded.
Pastoral staff	see *crozier*.
Paten	Plate for the consecrated bread at the *Eucharist*.
Pax	Small tablet kissed in turn by the congregation at the *Eucharist* in the Middle Ages, as a substitute for giving the kiss of peace to one another.
Pectoral cross	Small cross worn on the breast by bishops.
Pewter	Alloy of tin with copper (and lead in the cheaper kinds), used as substitute for silver. From the late seventeenth century some fine pewter contains antimony as a hardener. It was always made by casting.
Pome	A ball of metal, filled with hot coals to warm the priest's hands in church in cold weather.
Pyx	A container for the consecrated wafer bread known as the *Reserved Sacrament*.
Pyx, double	Has additional container for consecrated wine.
Pyx, hanging	Container for the *Reserved Sacrament*, suspended near the altar.
Recusants	English Roman Catholics in the sixteenth to eighteenth centuries, who refused to accept Protestantism or acknowledge the monarch as head of the Church of England.
Reformation	The break with the Church of Rome in the sixteenth century, by which Protestant Churches, including the Church of England, were set up.

Reserved Sacrament	Bread and wine consecrated at the *Eucharist*, kept for taking to the sick. They must be kept in a *pyx*, sometimes inside an *aumbry* or *tabernacle*.
Sacred Monogram	IHS, the first three letters of 'Jesus' in Greek.
Sacring Bell	Small bell rung at the moment of the consecration of bread and wine in the *Eucharist*.
Salver	Plate or dish set on a foot, used as a *paten* in the seventeenth and eighteenth centuries.
Sanctuary lamp	Hanging lamp kept burning near the altar, representing the presence of God or the *Reserved Sacrament*.
Sheffield Plate	A composite sheet metal, in which a layer of copper is sandwiched, by fusion, between two thin layers of silver. Used c.1760-1850.
Sick Communion sets	Made from the late eighteenth century onwards. Miniature sets of cup, *paten* and *flagon* or silver-topped bottle, used for taking the *Eucharist* in private houses for the sick.
Silver gilt	Gilded silver.
Standing paten, pyx etc	*Paten*, *pyx* etc. raised on a stem and a foot.
Sterling	The required standard of purity for silverware in the UK. It is 92.5% fine silver. See also *Britannia standard*.
Stocks for holy oil	See *ampullae*.
Stole	Scarf worn around the neck by a priest on its own or as part of *Eucharistic Vestments*.
Tabernacle	A housing on the altar, in which the *Reserved Sacrament* is kept.
Thurible	See *censer*.
Vernicle	Image of Christ's face on the cloth with which St Veronica wiped it on the way to the Crucifixion; often engraved on *patens*.
Waiter	Eighteenth-century household tray on feet, sometimes used as a *paten*.